Leellyn R. Suel
June 2018

Listening for Hope

A Few of Life's Poems

Leellyn Tuel

WESTBOW
PRESS®
A DIVISION OF THOMAS NELSON
& ZONDERVAN

WestBow Press books may be ordered through booksellers or by contacting:

WestBow Press
A Division of Thomas Nelson & Zondervan
1663 Liberty Drive
Bloomington, IN 47403
www.westbowpress.com
1 (866) 928-1240

THE HOLY BIBLE, NEW INTERNATIONAL VERSION®, NIV® Copyright © 1973, 1978, 1984, 2011 by Biblica, Inc.® Used by permission. All rights reserved worldwide.

Permission granted for author photo by Lifetouch National School Studios.

ISBN: 978-1-9736-2569-8 (sc)
ISBN: 978-1-9736-2570-4 (e)

Library of Congress Control Number: 2018904452

Print information available on the last page.

WestBow Press rev. date: 4/19/2018

DEDICATION

To my mother, Evelyn Ruth Schultz, who inspires
me to trust God and his promises

CONTENTS

Preface ix

   1.   The Beginnings of Hope....................................1

   2.   Nature Nurtures Hope..9

   3.   Changes Challenge Hope..................................23

   4.   Ponderings Produce Hope................................31

   5.   Praises Portray Hope..57

Acknowledgments 65

Notes 67

PREFACE

The first poem I ever wrote was this:

A little wee
including me
made us three
drinking talk
and coffee
well past three
or four.

I wrote it in college in 1973 for my elementary art professor, Don Robertson, in my final project, a collection of all the artwork we had done during the semester. Inspired by his creative spirit, I added poems that responded to each piece of art.

This means of expressing life lay dormant until 1990. My three children were all in grade school, and I had returned to teaching. The sudden challenges of a larger life drove me to a deeper walk with Jesus. Every morning, I cherished time reading my Bible, praying for help and insight, and journaling. Often those entries included poems that I heard in response to life and the trials I was facing.

My first significant trial came when I was nine. My family moved from Washington and the waves of Whidbey Island to the waving wheat of Oklahoma. The difficulty of making new friends and navigating a new culture created wounds of rejection and insecurity, which would flare up during future events when self worth or competence was being threatened.

The first major test of my adult life came with three children born in four years. My husband, Gene, and I became aware that Brian, the youngest, had multiple disabilities. I was stripped of the carefully constructed façade that I was the perfect Christian woman. I didn't have the energy to be good. We became deeply humbled by the truth that God does not need our competence to produce his power in our lives. When we are weak, then he makes us strong.

When all three children were in school, God opened up the opportunity to teach again. I had not seen this coming, but it was offered, and Gene said, "Why not? This is your training!" I soon found that it was what I was born for. Teaching gave me the treasure of nurturing a safe, creative universe each and every year, a place where children felt accepted and could develop amazing strengths.

The elementary school where I spent most of my career has a linguistically and culturally diverse population. As a result, I completed my ESL (English As a Second Language) endorsement, and this led to a further challenge: presenting a course in English teaching methods in Southeast Asia with Gene, who holds a master's degree in ESL. For 12 summers, for weeks at a time, I joined him in this endeavor. This was both exhausting and full of joys.

All of my adult life I have had a heart to encourage women, sharing God's words and his ways to give women hope for their situations. Every difficulty I've gone through has contributed perspective and comfort.

Weaving through all these stories is the thread of our marriage. Even though our shared values are strong and inviolable, our personality inventories put us at opposite ends of the spectrum for how we negotiate life.

So, in all these heart-stirring events, I listened to God, searching his face for words of hope and joy and wisdom. In my meditations, poems surfaced. I tucked them quietly away, these words known only by God and me. And then, some years ago, I went on a spiritual quest through those journal pages, reflecting on my path and compiling the poems into a collection. Holding my breath, I began sharing some of them with friends and family, who gave me enough positive feedback to sustain my dream of giving birth to a book.

Then, at the end of the school year in May 2015, I stood in my classroom – this creative universe – and promised my second-graders that I would publish my poetry. That promise has carried me to the shores where I now stand, waiting for the launch of this little ship christened *Listening for Hope*.

Leellyn Tuel
Lawrence, Kansas
March 2018

WHISPERS

May 2006

Fill your life with wonder,
And a poem will appear,
Peeking round a corner,
Whispering in your ear,
Rising up within you,
Distilling the wonder
In a whisper of words.

A POEM

Fall 2008

The power of a poem
is that
it makes you look up
    and far away
    and
    deep
    inside
and listen to the beauty.

The Beginnings of Hope

WELL PAST THREE

April 1973

A little wee,
including me,
made us three,
drinking talk
and coffee
well past three
or four.

SOME MORNINGS

April 1973

Some mornings have a habit
    of being deceitful.
They start out with a promise
    of sunshine and smiles
and slowly drag their unseen
    tail of dark troubles
round and above
    until the sunshine is only
    in your hand
and slowly falling apart.
Then it is fun to say "aha!"
    and run and run around and through
and past the forked tail and
fling the sunshine
    and stand under it
and wait,
    wait for the smile to follow.

SAGE

April 1973

A long time ago,
there came and happened
a most extraordinary and ancient sage.
He came among us,
    sat among us,
and after he had died,
he said hello.

TRUTH

April 1973

Such is truth, green and growing,
Peaceful to the eyes,
In an eternal billow of quiet blue.

SEA AT DAWN

April 1973

See the sea at dawn
in peace,
and ask him how
he is this day
before you venture
too near
and he licks your face.

Nature
Nurtures
Hope

FROM EARTH

January 1992

And in life is oft the theme:
from earth will come
the rose's bloom.

And so in times of little hope
and hearts that boast
    no special grace,
the blush of rose,
its fragrance full,
will bloom
and beauty will prevail.

THE BEACH

April 2003

Light-hearted feet
Traipsing down a
Mossy, forested tunnel
Emerge on the beach,
Our very own
Miles of beach.
Silky sand stretches forever,
Greeting us in the morning,
Tide splashing at our feet,
Sending us home at night
To dream of curiosity—
Wandering,
Wondering
At the ever-changing world
Where land meets sea
And will always be the same.

WAVES

Summer 2005

Waves are in my soul forever,
lapping, splashing
        at the edges of my memory,
sometimes crashing,
sometimes whispering,
always in the background,
the accompaniment
        to my dreams,
the faithfulness of God
        in their voice.

WHIDBEY ISLAND'S CHILD

December 2002

She grew up in a land of magic,
    a land safe and free and happy,
    bounded by meadows, evergreens,
    mossy cliff paths,
    and waves ever lapping at beaches.

Whidbey Island has her heart
    locked in a treasure chest
    somewhere under
    a tall, whispering evergreen
    among the ferns
    or hidden beneath the driftwood
    scattered along the edge of a beach.

CHRYSALIS

October 2008

It's hard to sustain fame
when you are now
   the chrysalis
     and the beauty
       has flown away.

WHIDBEY ISLAND

Spring 2008

My sisters went on a trip
without me

to the island
our hearts never left,

and they brought it back in a jar,
that world in a jar for me.
It is all as true as really there.

> Slimy, green-black kelp
>   smelling like the sea,
> a sand crab shell
>   echoing a scurry of legs,
> a mussel shell
>   abandoned,
> a finger of driftwood
>   reminiscent of playhouses created,
> the sand still wet from the bay,
> crusty barnacles
>   clinging to rocks, displaced,
> a second chunk of driftwood
>   hidden in the middle,
>   holding it all up,

and I can hear the waves
and smell the air
and I shiver,
and my toes are in the sand,
and I cry.
My sisters went on a trip without me,
but I was also there.
The salt is on my lips.

STRAWBERRIES

Spring 2008

Two red strawberries
saved for me
the essence of spring.
Hidden in the green of my garden,
nibbled on by something
that shares my backyard.
But the sweet, red surprise of spring
sat in my hand and
awakened me this morning.

OCEAN SONG

November 2016

The ocean always
Sings the steady heartbeat of God.
Its percussion is calling,
Rocking our senses
To listen and look for him
Beyond the crashing coastlines,
Carrying home the song to remember.

LEAVES

2017

My heart was gray,
the way forlorn
that cold November morn.

My path led past
a sheltering line
of silent trees,
now uncloaked and bare,
save for one.
She was too proud to release
her mantle of golden yellow,
but I would not have seen it
as I trudged downhearted below.

And now, apparently,
I have been expected.
The stage is set,
and I have entered.
For at this very moment
I catch a glint of
Yellow leaves pulled down, down, down.
Just now.

I lift my head
to find I stand
on the edge of the stage,
a shaft of soft light illuminating
the tree uncloaking.

It is holy ground
as every leaf adorning
the tree silently falls,
pulled down, down, slowly,
a cascade of lost beauty.
Every leaf in the space of a breath long held
creating a glittering carpet of gold.

The tree stands quite still,
as stunned as I,
and we take a long, slow smile
as we hear very clearly,
"Weep not for your leaves, tree.
The winter serves your beauty."

OCTOBER MORNING

2017

Dappled cheer
of a sunny October morning.

Always, always
the God of eternity
seeks my heart
and desires my friendship
    in the cross,
    in his care,
    in the stars,
    in the sea,
    in my friends,
    in my cares,
    in the inner voice,
    in my everywhere.

And in the dappled cheer
of a sunny October morning,

delight awakens delight.

GINGKO LEAVES

November 2017

The gingko leaves
    rest,
        scattered on my porch,
mingled with maple,
wooing tessellation dreams,
testament to graceful greatness,
        holding on to creamy green.

Changes
Challenge
Hope

A MILLION MILES

February 2002

In the child's heart
There was yet the crunch of morning sand,
The fresh ocean breezes,
The mighty rush of fir trees, their comforting canopy,
The deep smell of moss in her heart,
The thrill of crashing waves.

She was a refugee wandering in
     The flatlands of red dirt.
She was a million miles from friendship.

No one told her it could be home.
No one told her the children were lying.
     "You're not wanted here.
     You're not like us."
No one told her the whispering wheat
Spoke peace and calm,
The big unbroken sky
Echoed the greatness of God,
The endless flatness belied the great security.
She saw only endless boredom and loneliness.

BITTERNESS

January 2009

So many sorrows
    and so many ways to find
    his eyes, his tears, his arms,
    his refuge.
I can let this sorrow go.
    It is not and never was
    my Father's view
    that he was not there.
Did I not hear the whispers
    of his love and presence?
Not then.

When we moved to that dry and dusty and windy place,
    my life was turned upside down
    and shaken like a purse
        discarded.
    I was left empty,
    my old identity and self-sufficiency
        and importance
            gone.
I lay in bed in the little room
    far from the others
    on a wet pillow,
        sure I really could die
        and they would not
            care to know.
I was nine,
    and the world did not care.
And the seed of sorrow
concerning the incompetence of God's love
    was born.

I did not know
    God was tempering my soul
    and giving me compassion
    and blunting my pride
    and giving me an obsession for his presence and love.

RELEASE

March 2001

This ever child, though twenty-one,
    We are releasing
To find his way
    With others,

Sure we are abandoning
    Our mission
And afraid he will wonder
    Where we are in the night.

Sure we are
    That he must find freedom
And that we must find rest
    In the Shepherd who will keep him near.

THE END

January 2018

The days till the end
of life as I've known it
stand on the kitchen calendar,
four months
till the day
I walk away.

The next four months
wait for the imaginary future
to chart the course
ready to be written
for the launch of
the next unknown me.

THE PRINCESS SUFFERS

February 20, 2018

I'm working with the script
    that I've been given.
He changed it out
    and gave no reason.

He gave the role of servant
    and took away the cape and crown,
to live quietly as second
    and live as he, for no renown.

They sweep the set;
    there's no part for me to play.
I catch my breath.
    I am alone at end of day.

The princess suffers,
    truth be told,
but hold your pity.
    She will come forth as gold.

*My sheep listen to my voice; I know them,
and they follow me. John 10:27 NIV*

Ponderings
Produce
Hope

MY WORLD

March 2003

The world lives
    in my classroom,
and I am the leader
    of the little mob.
How God can do it
    I scarce can tell,
ruling his world with all its complexity.
I can barely manage
one little warring heart
that threatens to destroy
our carefully trained unity.

So, my Father, King of the universe,
for whom ruling is an art
    accomplished well,
I come to you seeking advice.
I need your diplomacy
    and your miraculous ways
to bring order and peace and purpose
to my little warring world.

WHERE IS HOPE?

2004

When a country is at odds with the universe?
When financial monsters threaten to strangle a school system?
When a church endures years of unresolved and public conflicts and splits?
When misunderstanding and standoff rocks relationships?
When one's out of options to help a friend caught in a cycle of tragedies?

Where is hope and where is
    "Seated in the heavenly realms"[1] and
    "Abundant life" and
    "Knowing the depths of Jesus's love
        Wide and long and high and deep"[2] and
    "Filled to all the fullness of God?"[3]

I urgently want resolutions and growth and smiles and handshakes all around,
But the scope of my prayers
Are stretched beyond measure.
The limit of my understanding
    Of God's wisdom,
My vulnerability, is exposed and threatened
    By forces that apparently can't be tamed.

How long, O Lord?
I echo a question of biblical proportion.
Where are you?
Are we forsaken?
Is my faith only meant for
    Church pews,
    Morning devotions,
    Spiritual stress relief?

        I remember faintly
            A bigger answer that matters
            And makes a difference,
        But not today,
            In these hours
        With rocks in my heart,
            sinking me
                to the bottom.

MY LITTLE HEART

October 2006

My little heart
    turns to people not God,
    craving their assent.
O God, free me for you.

    I am for you.
    I want to be
        what you want to see.
    At home with you,
        my restless obsessions
        subsiding.

PSALM 42,43

October 2006

My heart is battered
by my senses in this real world,
breathless
with the demands of my real world.

The image of your invisibility
and all its promise
wavers in my real heart.
I yearn for hope and strength and comfort
only to hear them echo
in the fog.

And yet,
I wait for the sun to rise.

THE CLIMB

June 2007

The climb looms ahead,
an adventure
that will test our
meager limits.

However,
we still live
in God's realm.
He is here,
    extending a hand up
    and provisions to endure
    and signposts along the way
to bring us to the top,
and we will plant our flag at the end.

TAPESTRY

March 2008

The tapestry of my life
    is woven in grey
    at this end
    in this space.
The windows are
    drawn tight.
The doors are closed.
The sky is low.
There are no bright colors
    or light gleaming.
But yet I'm hearing
    The pathos of
    "Seven Wonders of the World, Temple of Artemis"
    playing in the background.

INTEGRITY

January 2008

God, make me real.
    Bring integrity.
I feel like an image out of focus.
    There are two of me projected;
    some parts overlap.
But
who decides the focus?
Who names reality?

II CORINTHIANS 12:9,10

November 2007

Small as I am,
Weak as I am,
    Over and over
    I stumble and fall.
Small as I am,
Weak as I am,
    You touch my hand,
    And I matter to you.
Small as I am,
Weak as I am,
    Great things are done
    As I love in your name.
There is only one song.
There will always be only one song:
    Christ in me,
    Christ alone.

WORDS

September 2004

As with a good many politicians
I've said a good many things in my life
that,
given another chance
and another character,
I'd rather have said
a good bit differently.

WATCHING

October 2008

My friend is engulfed
   in a Tolkien-size
   dark struggle
      through cold, deep snow
      and dark forests,
   bearing a flickering light
   of hope
      against overwhelming odds
with an unwieldy burden
      and a flickering heartbeat
      dragging behind,
   sometimes pushing ahead,
   sometimes sliding and tumbling
      down scree.
The burden strangles her
   with ropes
   tangling her feet.

And yet,
scraped, bruised, breathless,
she plods on.
Deep within she guards
   a hope in
   the maker of her quest
   and his love,
not quite sure of
   the direction or the map,
but founded on eternity sure
and the portal at the end.

There love will prove
   to have been the other anchor
   tied around her waist.

THE MASK

November 2008

My mask
is getting brittle
and translucent.

I'm pasting another smile on.
I'm putting on the glasses
    with JOY stamped
    on each lens.
I'm scrawling PEACE across my forehead.

Looking intently in your face
    for readings on my worth
    and my score,
keeping a daily tally of affirmations,
I reel and spin
    when I catch a glazed eye,
    a frown.

Yet when I emerge from the chrysalis
I shall be
    sincere,
    secure,
    and caring.

PSALM 73

August 2008

I went to a feast
and nibbled on my crackers
  under the table.

I went to the opening ceremonies
of the Beijing Olympics
and played solitaire
  in a hallway.

I went to Mannheim Steamroller
and didn't get out of my car,
so I could listen to "Wee Sing."

I went to the Grand Canyon
and colored in a coloring book.

Oh, God, heaven has only One,
And what on earth
Can stir my passions?

I must not miss
  this best of all feasts,
  this best of all performances,
  this best of all glories.

FREE

February 2008

All the terrors
that want to be mine
stand outside the door,
waiting,
waiting
to be frisked
by Jesus
and stripped of their weapons.

I might let them in,
but I trust Jesus
to stand at the door.

REFLECTIONS IN AN AIRPORT

March 2009

The grandma's warm smile
regarding the screaming child
savors the sweet past.

ON A MOUNTAINSIDE

March 2009

The contorted tree
with unconquerable pain
gives unique beauty.

THREE TREES

May 2012

There was a tree
where Jesus died to set us free
from who we are
and who we aren't.

The wounds. The hurt.
The despair and sorrow.
They knew he was the Messiah,
and now this.

The storm rumbled and howled,
echoing their hearts adrift.
But Glory surprised them all
and redeemed the impossible.
They had not foreseen
resurrection.

An earlier tree was
the reason for this Glory.
Two had chosen
what they shouldn't,
and they were driven out of their Eden
in a whirlwind of drama.
But Glory and Grace
trumped the impossible
and promised a Redeemer.

And we feel it all now
condensed in the swirling
despair and hope
in the storm around Cleo's fatal tree
as we lose our breath thinking
of what we lost
and what we shall gain.
There is a promise
whispering through the wind.

No tree is final.
The impossible
bows to the One above the storm.

HOPE

October 2012

Romans 8:28, Ephesians 3:20

There's nothing like a Great Problem
When it meets the Great Problem-Solver.
Uh-uh. There's nothing at all, all night long.
As you think on it,
You can start to hear the singing.
You can hear those angels singing,
"Holy, holy, Great God Almighty,
Do what you want to do all the time!"
Yes, indeed, those Great Problems
Sure are wonderful opportunities
To see the surprises of God.
Your heart just sings to think of how
His power and goodness
Are sure to break through!

WELCOME TROUBLE AS FRIENDS

March 2013

James 1:2-4

Life introduces itself
In a new form,
Magnificent and terrifying
In proportion to my present form.

I clutch the railing
Above the yawning precipice
Where we have met,
Praying against the foe I face.

But through the mist
And howling winds,
Perception takes a hopeful turn:
Masks make foes appear as friends.

The waves still crash;
The overwhelming force will threaten.
But the masks will
Trump the danger they ride upon.

Mindbender advances
With steely eyes
To give me broader scope
Than I had surmised.

I take his hand
And welcome him.
He lifts me up; he makes me stand.
I see the way, no longer dim.

Heartbender shows her true face,
Settled peace and not confusion,
Melding the lives of my people
Into deeper and freer union.

I take her hand
And welcome her.
She lifts me up; she makes me stand.
I feel my heart opening and my motives purifying.

The mask of Soulmaker shines,
Pulsing with a grand story,
The deepest battles, close and far,
Are to shape eternity's glory.

I take his hand.
I welcome him.
He lifts me up; he makes me stand,
I know the depths of love. Amen.

And to you, O God Almighty,
I bring them all,
Hand in hand.
Before your feet we fall.

You gave the trials, masked as friends,
Redeeming life.
I take your hand;
I welcome you.

DAISIES AND THORNS

June 2017

Daisies gracing
The garden
Don't make up for
Thorns in the house.

WORDS

July 2017

Raw wounds moan on the soul
From words that are cold.

Scraped flesh screaming
So it can bring healing.

THANKFULNESS

July 2017

Thankfulness daily rings my
    doorbell
    and waits.
Today I peek through the
    curtains to see if
    she has gone.
    But, no,
    she is now sitting
    on the front step,
    waiting yet.
I grit my teeth
    and go about
    my duties,
    distracted by Thankfulness
    quietly, persistently inviting
    me to welcome her.
I go to bed quite aware
    I have been
    a wretched neighbor
    shutting my heart
    to her goodwill.
I have no cause
    to criticize
    for she has full right
    to her request.
At first hint of dawn
    before demands have begun,
    I go to the window
    to see if she has abandoned me.
And, oh!
    She has managed
    a comfortable porch swing
    under the tree.
So, quickly,
    to match the rhythm of my heart,
    I brew a pot of tea
    to share.

THE THRONE

August 2017

Floundering in the dark,
pressed and haunted
by my insufficiencies and failures,
I was on my knees
rooted at bedside
in a free fall of despair and prayer.

I cradled my mind in one arm
and reached for God's hand with the other.
I finally made it past the enemy's taunts
to the Throne Room
where the Almighty Father
rules all things great and small,
far-flung and near.
I must see his mind and feel his heart
to anchor my sanity, hoping for his mercy and help.

I stand back, holding my breath, and I watch.
I agree with the angels
as I can only imagine they have already asked,
"Why did you not ask us to nudge her
to prevent this mistake?"

And I knew, I saw in his eyes,
that He Who easily manages
all the details and balance to the far reaches replied,
"Oh, no, I wanted her to learn to trust me
and know my love and have my peace
in seeing how I redeem impossible things."

And finally, my heart rested,
and I slept in peace.

Praises
Portray
Hope

DEEPER THAN FRACTAL GEOMETRY
MATHEMATICS ECHOES ETERNITY

1990

When eternity
entered time
and touched
the minutiae
of our planet,
    the complexity,
    the infinity,
    the magnificence
    of God
exploded in our view,

because
the smaller one becomes,
the more complex
    and glorious
    it all becomes.

THE MELODRAMA OF THE COSMOS

August 2000

To save my soul

broke the heart of heaven.

Love and death

mended the chasm.

THE GREAT EPIC

November 2001

Before all stories,
Before all authors,
There was God.
He started a story for us
That's true,
True,
True,
That spans eternity,
And we are in it.

The great and Almighty God of eternity
Made a race,
And settled them
In a little planet
In a corner of the Milky Way.

In their smallness
They filled his great heart
With love and delight.
His character was revealed
In their creation.
And so in their great importance
And in his great love
        Two things happened

They ruined it all,
        Thinking they alone could run it all,
        And erased God from their sky.
And he in his love
Planned a marvelous,
Unimaginable plan to transform their ruin
And restore the love between them.

He himself concentrated himself into
    Their small world
And became Jesus, that side of himself
    That would show them his heart
    In a way they could see.

The great and almighty creative soul
    Of the universe
Went into the abyss
    To recapture our love.
He alone had the power
To overcome the ruin
And set us free
So we again could
See his true heart.

And in a stroke of genius
The Great and Almighty God
    Put his heart
    In the small ones
    Who saw what Jesus had done
And knew it was true.

And so they will remain,
    Bonded in loyalty
    To Him forever,
    Surpassing their smallness,
    Released from the bonds of their planet,
    And tasting the greatness of love,
    Living forever great in God's eternity.

And the whole planet
From core to mountaintop
Bursts with wonder
That such a story is true.

THIS PLANET, EPHESIANS 2:10

February 2004

Our planet sings
The reverberations of grace,
Bringing glory to God
In the farthest reaches
Of the universe.

The smallest ripple
Of redemption and righteousness
In our hearts,
In our work,
In our churches,
In our world
Is felt by angels out there.

And they sing,
"Hallelujah!
They're believing You!
They're seeing past the barrier!"

They turn in awe to the
Lord of heaven and earth.
He is greater than they knew.

HIS GLORY

January 2018

The heavens declare
A Heart moves a Hand to show
His glory so clear.

ACKNOWLEDGMENTS

I am thankful for Westbow Press's technical staff, whose gracious assistance lowered the hurdle for the complexities of self-publishing.

I am grateful for family and countless friends who have partnered with me in growing in our faith over the years. Your encouragement and examples have given me strength.

Jyl, thank you for being my lifelong friend and showing up nearly every Friday morning to share and pray through life before our days began. Your constant belief in me gave me courage.

Megan and Jesse, I am honored to be your mother. Your support has meant so much as you watched me grow up alongside you. Brian, even though you have no words, I acknowledge that you have spoken to us of eternal things. Nathan and Stacy, you have enriched us and made us more real, and we cannot imagine better in-laws.

Gene, for 46 years now, you have lifted my chin to make me look to the Lord. I remember when we were engaged, you would have me say, "I love Jesus more than Gene." This was, and is, priceless. I honor you for giving me room to follow the Lord and my dreams.

NOTES

CHAPTER 4: Ponderings Produce Hope

1. Ephesians 2:6, NIV
2. Ephesians 3:18, NIV
3. Ephesians 3:19, NIV